THE SIMPLE LIFE

GUIDE TO RV LIVING

Other Books by Gary Collins

The Simple Life Guide To Optimal Health: *How to Get Healthy and Feel Better Than Ever*

The Simple Life Guide To Decluttering Your Life: *The How-To Book of Doing More with Less and Focusing on the Things That Matter*

Going Off The Grid: *The How-To Book of Simple Living and Happiness*

Living off the Grid: *What to Expect While Living the Life of Ultimate Freedom and Tranquility*

The Beginners Guide To Living Off The Grid: *The DIY Workbook for Living The Life You Want*

For a complete and updated list of *The Simple Life* book series and other books by Gary Collins, go to **www.thesimplelifenow.com**

THE SIMPLE LIFE

GUIDE TO RV LIVING

The Road to Freedom and
the Mobile Lifestyle Revolution

GARY COLLINS, MS

The Simple Life Series (Book 1)

The Simple Life Guide to RV Living:
The Road To Freedom and the Mobile Lifestyle Revolution

First Edition

Printed in the United States of America

Copyright ©2018

Published by Second Nature Publishing, Albuquerque, NM 87109

For information about special discounts for bulk purchasing, and/or direct inquiries about copyright, permission, reproduction and publishing inquiries, please contact Book Publishing Company at 888-260-8458.

DISCLAIMER OF WARRANTY

The intent of this material is to further educate you in the area of the mobile living lifestyle.

The text and other related materials are for informational purposes only. The data, author's opinions, and information contained herein are based upon information from various published and unpublished sources that represent the mobile living lifestyle and practice summarized by the author and publisher. Even though the author has been as thorough as possible in his research, the publisher of this text makes no warranties, expressed or implied, regarding the currency, completeness, or scientific accuracy of this information, nor does it warrant the fitness of the information for any particular purpose. Any claims or presentations regarding any specific products or brand names are strictly the responsibility of the product owners or manufacturers. This summary of information from unpublished sources, books, research journals, articles, and the author's opinions are not intended to replace the advice or recommendations by professionals.

Due to the great variability of people living mobile lifestyles, and so forth, the author and Second Nature Publishing assume no responsibility for personal injury, property damage, or loss from actions inspired by information in this book. Always consult professionals first. When in doubt, ask for advice. Recommendations in this book are no substitute for the directives of professionals, manufacturers, or federal, state, and local regulatory officials.

ISBN 978-1-57067-363-4

Get Your Free
Goodies and Stuff!

Building a solid relationship with my readers is very important to me. It is one of the rewards of being a writer. From time to time, I send out my newsletter (never spammy, I promise) to keep you up to date with special offers and information about anything new I may be doing.

If that's not enough enticement, when you sign up for my newsletter I'll send you some spectacular free stuff!

1. A list of all the travel trailer and mobile living resources that I own and personally use. I guarantee this will save you a ton of time, money, and headaches.

2. The first chapter of my best selling book *Going Off The Grid*.

3. My going-off-the-grid resource list—again critical for those who are pursuing, or interested in living, a more remote lifestyle.

You can get all the goodies above by signing up for my mailing list at: www.thesimplelifenow.com/mobileresources.

TABLE OF CONTENTS

INTRODUCTION

What Is This Book About?

While living and running my business remotely out of my travel trailer, I've noticed there are a lot of online forums and websites dedicated to the lifestyle but not a whole lot of books on the topic. As you all know, I write about the things I have personally experienced and what others have shown interest in as it relates to my life. This book was born of my experience, both the failures, and the successes.

In this book I will cover the basics on how to get started living a mobile lifestyle. I'll share what I have found to be the best products to set up such a lifestyle. Believe me, I made a bunch of mistakes in the beginning, but after a lot of trial and error, I figured out what I feel works and will work best for most people. My goal is to pass this information on to you, so you don't have to make the same mistakes. I hope to help you jump into the lifestyle more quickly and easily than I did.

As with all of my books, I must emphasize that this is just a guide. The type of mobile lifestyle you choose and how far you want to take it is completely up to you. Just because something worked for me, doesn't mean it will work or be a good fit for you. Hey, this is an adventure, right? You don't have to make these changes the way I did. In fact, I hope you don't do it just like me; find your own path and do it your own way!

MOBILE LIVING DEFINED

For simplicity, when talking about travel trailers, tiny homes, fifth-wheels, or motorized recreational vehicles, I will use the term RV. Don't worry, later in this book I will give you a full explanation on all the different types and categories of recreational vehicles, but just remember, when I say RV, I'm talking about all the terms listed above.

Recently there has been a renaissance in living a more simple and mobile lifestyle. RVs and mobile homes have been around for over a hundred years, but people are rediscovering these types of dwellings in an effort not to feel stuck or rooted in one place. In the past, these types of homes earned a negative stigma associated with poor people or squatters. How times have changed!

Today people are looking for ways to be more mobile. We don't all want to live in one place. Instead, many of us choose to move around and experience more of a "nomadic" lifestyle. Not too long ago, before the advent of agriculture and animal domestication, humans were hunter-gatherers. What did that mean? For hundreds of thousands of years, it was a lifestyle that dictated that humans continually move in order to find consistent food sources. Humans had learned that if they stayed in one place too long, they would eventually run out of food. The reason? It's logical: you are hunting the animals and eating all the vegetation in the area before it can replenish. Not only that, but animals are not that stupid in the wild; eventually, they figure out to stay away from humans to avoid getting eaten! The solution? Carry all your belongings on your back and hit the road. That means that the first automobiles were our feet, and the first travel trailer was a backpack probably made of deerskin or some other animal hide.

We don't live as the early nomads did anymore. These days, with the advancements of new safer and lighter materials, we can live a very comfortable, mobile lifestyle—and it costs far less than buying a house in today's economy. I truly enjoy my new lifestyle; I wish I had found it sooner.

Over the last couple of years, while documenting my *Going Off The Grid* project and then publishing the book that followed, I have received a lot of questions about mobile living. As my loyal followers know, I have been living in my travel trailer for several years while building my off-the-grid home. Not only that, but I have also been traveling south away from my off-the-grid house during the cold winter months. As a result of all this nomadic movement, I run my business completely remotely. Needless to say, people observing my journey always want to know how I'm living this type of life and how I was able to get started.

People are very tuned in to DIY shows, remodels, and tiny home builds. The tiny home bonanza is in full swing as I write this, but getting hidden in the tiny home trend is the traditional RV lifestyle that was made famous by retirees exploring the country with their newfound freedom. Both tiny homes and traditional RVs have a place in this mobile lifestyle, but I sense a lot of confusion about what each of these mobile types of homes offer. Let's see if we can determine which one is best for you.

I would not recommend just jumping into a mobile lifestyle without thinking it through. This is a dramatic paradigm shift away from "traditional living" as know today. There are a ton of blogs suggesting you purchase a beat-up van or RV, hit the road, and see what happens. You *can* do it that way, and more power to you if you can make it work, but I would say finding success in hitting the road without preparation is definitely the exception and not the rule.

There are many things you must consider before making this life choice. Hopefully, my journey and this book will be of great benefit for those looking to take the leap.

1

My Story: How My Mobile Lifestyle Began

DEALING WITH TODAY'S LIFE GRIND

As most of you who follow me or have read my book *Going Off The Grid* know, my journey didn't start as a whim. I constructed the foundation of how I live today about 10 years ago. It started as a desire to live more remotely and simply, then it evolved into a complete lifestyle change.

First, I think it is important to understand that I grew up in a small town in the mountains of California, so living off the grid in the Pacific Northwest is not as drastic a stretch for me as one might think. I did not go into this adventure completely in the dark.

During my life, I have lived in many cities across the country. As I have aged, I have become more disenchanted with and disengaged from that type of living. Urban living is not a bad lifestyle; it's just not for me anymore.

Having grown up poor in a single-wide trailer, you would think

I would not ever want to return to such a lifestyle. That couldn't be farther from the truth. Having grown up that way has given me a different perspective on what I truly think is important. Sure, at times things were tough growing up, but it made me appreciate everything I had that much more. I now look back and consider myself incredibly lucky to have had these experiences. I was fortunate enough to know most of the people in my town. I was able to wave at them and get a wave back in return. That is pretty much unheard of in an urban setting today.

I still have fond memories of racing home from football practice before the sun went down to get in an hour of bird hunting. Heck, I would have my shotgun behind the seat of my truck to save time. Yes, that would mean I had a shotgun on school grounds, and I wouldn't have been the only one. Most of us were hunters, and that was just all there was to it. Can you imagine what would happen to a kid doing that today?

Once I left for college at eighteen, I had very few opportunities to do the things I enjoyed doing while growing up—hiking, fishing, hunting . . . just being in nature. For many years I had yearned to return to that type of living. It is hard to explain to someone who has never experienced this lifestyle, but for me, spending time outdoors always made me the happiest.

To me, the daily grind of living in congested areas has become completely overwhelming and too stressful. Why would I want to sit in traffic if I don't have to? The thought of going to the mall actually makes me cringe to say the least.

Now I can't state this enough: there was a lot of planning with numerous false starts and mistakes made along the way. With that being said, I wouldn't change a thing. Well, maybe I wish someone had already written the books I have put together, as it would have made my life much easier.

Like most people today, I was doing the day-to-day grind and had spent almost half my life working for the government in one form or another. Needless to say, I was completely burned out and was questioning numerous aspects of my life. I remember just sitting there at my desk, after another joyless meeting with one of my bosses, thinking, *What the heck am I doing with my life?* Now, I knew I needed a plan, but what *was* that plan? I had a house that was ridiculously expensive, with more debt than I wanted or was really necessary, and I was living in congested Southern California slowly losing my mind.

I know now that the dissatisfaction with my previous lifestyle and mindset is not an unusual sentiment. I remember thinking, "Is there something wrong with me?"

I have spoken to and received emails from hundreds and hundreds of people who feel exactly as I do. If you feel this way, you are not alone. Today there a lot more groups who are looking for, or actually living, the same type of lifestyle I live today. Simply put, we are not willing to accept the modern-day societal expectation that we grind ourselves to oblivion chasing someone else's predefined idea of happiness . . . there has to be a better way!

The Search Begins . . . Kind Of

The original plan just simply started; I wanted to find someplace quiet to get away. So I started looking at remote land or cabins in Oregon, Washington, Wyoming, and Montana. It was just a cursory look. As it was in the middle of the housing boom, I soon noticed that remote properties were just as overpriced as the typical family dwelling in more populated areas. I called a couple realtors just to get some information, but nothing serious came of it. Needless to say, I was a little discouraged that my plan was nothing more than a dream.

I shelved my plan and continued with my daily grind, discouraged. What I have found, after over a decade of research, is that everyone goes through this type of discouragement.

Another important point I need to make is I have never fit into the mold of today's American lifestyle: the nine-to-five job, the commute, the cookie-cutter suburban home. I started my own side business a good ten years prior to hatching my idea of a mobile lifestyle in an effort to break out. I have always been more of a "free thinker." I knew that in order to really have freedom, I would have to run not only my own life but also my own business. Let me assure you, though, I don't think it is 100 percent necessary for you to run your own business to live a more mobile lifestyle, but it sure helps. The best advice I can give is if you are feeling the grind and really serious about living a simpler or more mobile lifestyle, you need to come up with a business model that fits this type of lifestyle.

A Kick in the Butt—The Real Search Begins

Fast forward to 2013, and all these thoughts were still in the back of my mind. But due to many life-changing circumstances, I wasn't really pursing my dream; I was in a rut. In that year, the stress of trying to run my own business weighed on me and numerous recent deaths of loved ones, including one of my best friends, hit home. I knew if I kept saying, "I will get to it next year," it would never happen.

So with that, I rekindled the dream and put a plan into action. From the time when I had originally thought about living a simpler, more remote lifestyle, my ideas had evolved and changed. I had started a new business, sold my house and most of my belongings, and was debt free. I was in a much better place to really pursue my dream. My original plan was to have a remote getaway; now it was to live off the grid for at least part of the year, dedicating myself to being more mobile rather than stuck in one place. I was fortunate while working in the government to have traveled all over the world, and found this traveling lifestyle a bit addictive. I had caught the nomadic bug—I realized I just couldn't stay in one place for very long. In addition, the housing bubble had taught me that the supposed American dream of home ownership—with that big fat mortgage—is a chain around the ankle of a freedom-based lifestyle.

Most think that living a mobile lifestyle or living off the grid means living in a beat-up van, cave, or shack with no running water or electricity. Today that couldn't be further from the truth. You can now live a comfortable life on a piece of fairly isolated land or travel around in a state-of-the-art RV. I know this for a fact! Not only am I doing it, but I have run into more people than I can count who are doing the same thing or something very similar.

OK, I am going to address this now, as it is the main argument I get from people who think what I do is not obtainable for most people because I'm single with no kids. I could go into a long diatribe about life decisions and lifestyle choices, but I will not—maybe in another book. (Haha, just kidding.)

The fact is I have met so many people who are married with two to three kids, not to mention multiple pets, who are living *exactly* like I am. I'm telling you with firsthand knowledge, *anyone can live this lifestyle successfully if they want to.* It all boils down to whether you want it and can make it happen proactively or whether you just want to make excuses and complain about your life. Yes, it's a little tough love, but someone has to say it. This life is as simple as coming up with a plan and putting it into action, instead of waiting for a miracle to happen, which will more than likely never occur.

I think the best part of this adventure is I'm funding it in a way that most American's can afford. I do not come from a long list of millionaires, and I do not have unlimited resources. Still, I won't deny, it does cost money, especially in the beginning. I know there are shows and books that say you can just take off with a hundred bucks in your pocket and do it. And some people have done it that way, but I like to live in reality and talk about what is plausible for *most* people not a selective few.

Hopefully you will enjoy my adventure, and even if you are not interested in such a lifestyle, maybe you will learn a little something that you can incorporate into your life to make it simpler and more enjoyable.

2

So Where Do You Start?
You Have Too Much Crap!

When you are thinking about living a more mobile lifestyle or even contemplating simplifying your life, I think you need a solid starting point. As I preach in my other books, it is always better to have a plan and to take it slow in the beginning. Many people caught up in our society's instant-gratification thought process forget that great things come with time and perseverance.

As you now know, my off-the-grid life and journey of simplification started several years ago when I decided to downsize. After owning several homes that were much bigger than I needed and filled with crap that I would never use, I decided it was time for a change.

The bottom line is, if you are truly interested in this type of lifestyle, you are going to have to downsize . . . and for most of you, you'll have to downsize a lot! There are some big RVs out there, but I can guarantee that not even a fraction of your current stuff is going to fit into the biggest ones on the market. Not to mention, the bigger the RV is, the more it is going to cost and the harder it will be to move from place to place.

CONSUMER NATION: BUYING EVERYTHING IN SIGHT DOESN'T EQUAL HAPPINESS

Just like most people today, I had spent my life being just what society and the system wanted me to be: the ultimate consumer. It's no secret that our lives suffer under maximum workloads in order to make money so that we can buy as much as we can to fill the unhappiness void. Now, I'm not saying there is no value in work, and I don't begrudge working hard and earning an honest wage, but I do think we have our priorities way out of whack today.

Why do we purchase the biggest house we can obtain and shackle ourselves to its suffocating loan? Why do we buy that sports car we really can't afford? Why do we have a closet full of clothes and shoes we hardly wear? In the end, we stress ourselves out so we can obtain all these items, and for what? Exactly! You can't answer that question because there is no logical or reasonable answer.

To me the answer is simple. We do all the above, and drive ourselves crazy in the process, because that is what we have been told to do in order to find happiness. So in today's society, stuff equals happiness. Trust me, I followed this mantra with gusto, purchasing all kinds of junk I didn't need.

Stop Being a Crap Collector

So where do you start? Well, just like any addict, admit you have a problem. I like to attribute the moniker *junkaholic* to the affliction most of us suffer from today. As a human, it might seem like your primary goal in life is to compile as much useless stuff as you can, and then die among the heaps of your ingloriously obtained items in the hopes that someone finds you before one of your pets starts eating your face. OK, I know that's a little over the top, but I think you see my point.

Just as I said above, the starting point is realizing that your life means more than your stuff. It would be further fulfilled by creating experiences rather than by acquiring shiny items. The luster of objects lasts for a very short time, then you need another shiny object to fill its void.

For me, I just had to realize that less was more. Just like my optimal health philosophy, the interpretation of *less* will be different for each individual. Having a more mobile life will mean keeping your house but having a getaway, or selling your house and renting, or going on occasional adventures in an RV, or building a tiny home, or going all-in and living year-round in an RV and traveling as much as possible. As for me, I wanted to live in a comfortable, up-to-date home off the grid but also spend part of the year going on adventures towing a travel trailer. In other words, less junk, fewer headaches, and more time for what truly matters in life . . . while still living in the modern world part-time. I knew I wouldn't be able to do this if I held onto a bunch of useless crap; I had to make a choice.

The starting point for me was to greatly downsize my living space. Back then, I was paying a ridiculous mortgage for a 1,700-square-foot house in Southern California and losing sleep constantly trying to figure out how to pay for it. I was single and had two dogs. Why I thought I needed this much space, even today, is a mystery to me. Well, not really. I had been brainwashed into thinking bigger was better. In the end, all it did was stress me out, financially and emotionally, and make me spend a great deal of time on upkeep when I could have been using that time doing something I truly enjoyed.

That is one important point I want to make about our modern maximum-consumption lifestyle: instead of making us happy, in the end, it actually makes us less happy and takes time away from our true passions and those individuals we care about. If that isn't true irony, I don't know what is. We spend a great deal of our lives pursuing the things that we have been told will make us happy, but in the end, they make us miserable and unfulfilled. Wow, the joke is on us. The great news is that we can change this, and I want to share with you my experience, and the steps you can take in order to *happify* (my made-up word) and simplify!

EVALUATE YOUR CURRENT LIVING CONDITIONS

The first thing you need to analyze is your current living situation. Can you get by with less living space? I would say almost everyone in this country could answer this with a resounding *yes*! If you live in a standard-size American house, and you say *no*, I'm pretty sure this mobile lifestyle is not for you. But at the same time, that doesn't mean you can't take this information, and downsize to a more affordable, smaller house. I know this book is primarily about mobile and RV living, but I'm a big believer in life simplification in general.

At the very least, I want people to look at RVs as a tool of freedom to get out and explore. Just because you don't follow in my footsteps doesn't mean that you will get nothing out of this book. My material will also cover RV basics, which is great for people who just want to get started and hit the road.

The first thing I did was simple: I analyzed my monthly cost of living expenses. This included my mortgage, insurance, utilities, and general upkeep expenses. It came out to an astounding $3,500 a month.

For those of you who do not live in California, or one of the more expensive states, you are probably flabbergasted by that amount. Let me tell you, that is cheap in Southern California. Most people I know in California easily spend around $5,000 to $6,000 or more, for what I outlined above. Now that I look back with my "what is important to me" clarity, this was absolutely nuts.

For me, I still had about twenty-seven years left on my mortgage, so that meant I could look forward to spending a total of $1,134,000 (yes, that is over a million dollars) if I maintained that type of lifestyle for the remainder of my mortgage. Here is the kicker: Most of us don't maintain, we upgrade. So for most of us, that total would actually go up.

Basically, we all have the capability of being millionaires if we just adjusted our lifestyle choices. That is a pretty astounding statement. Just thinking of the average person I know in California, their total would be close to double mine. I hope you are starting to see the insanity of our consumer-based economy in this country.

Most of you might think my example is rather dramatic, but I assure you, once I got settled in my new, down-sized place, it was anything but. As I outlined, I was living in the typical Southern California residential neighborhood in a home with three bedrooms, two bathrooms, and a two-car garage. For a single guy, this is just way too much space. Heck, I think it is too big for the average family, and I will explain why later.

Is Renting an Option?

The reason I bring up renting as an option is because it is a good transition if you are a homeowner who is planning to sell. Renting gives you a go-between while you downsize and get your plan together, but it avoids your having to make a big leap. It's getting your toes wet, wading into a simpler life in a smaller dwelling.

Obviously, you don't want to rent a place the same size or bigger than what you have already; you have to downsize, which will force you to get rid of the dogs-playing-poker print on the wall in that dusty man cave.

That being said, I do know people who skipped this step, sold the house and all their stuff, purchased an RV, and never looked back. Again this all comes down to your goals and lifestyle plans.

After analyzing how much my house cost each month, I decided to take a look at renting and see what made sense. I realized I needed time to get my finances in order, work further on my business, and finalize my plan to simplify my life. The first place I checked out was on Craigslist.com. I will tell you, it was very discouraging in the beginning; renting in California is fairly expensive when compared with the rest of the country. As I write this, another housing boom is overtaking California, and the prices are even higher than the previous one. I guess some of us never learn from the past.

Not to mention, back when I was looking to rent, it was just after the housing bubble had burst (the start of the Great Recession), so everyone was trying to do what I was doing. The glut of prospective renters was pushing rents even higher. The icing on the cake was having two large dogs; most rental owners really don't like pets, and if they do accept them, they almost always hit you with a significant up-charge.

So what did that mean? Instead of renting in my general location, I had to cast a wider net in order to find more options. Having pets meant I had to look in more rural areas where people didn't really care as much about renting to people who have pets. I started by looking for two-bedroom places, and quickly realized the price difference between what I was currently paying and the prospective rental was not large enough to justify this choice.

This forced me to start looking outside my perceived comfort zone. I began investigating studios, granny flats (small apartments attached to houses), and cottages (basically a studio house in which all living space is concentrated in one area as with a studio apartment).

This search opened an entirely new lifestyle that I had never experienced before; it simplified living far more than what I was used to. It is amazing: having less space forces you to have less stuff, which ultimately makes you happier. I'll be honest I really didn't see that happening in the beginning of my search.

Sometimes you might get lucky and find the place you want right away, but from my experience, making such a drastic change takes time. Here is why:

- Unless you have lived this way before, these could be neighborhoods or dwellings you have never experienced before.

- You will probably have to search in new areas with which you are unfamiliar and determine which works best for you current situation.

Here is the key (I have discussed this in some of my YouTube videos and other blog posts): Change is always painful in the beginning, and there is no getting around this. You have to realize you are making a major life change, and it is going to be uncomfortable. All great things in life come with some scrapes and bruises along the way.

My search for a rental home in Southern California took several months—six to be exact. I did a lot of research and soul-searching during this period and, ultimately, it paid off. I found a cottage with a full-size yard located in a rural part of San Diego.

In the end, by being patient, it ended up being the nicest place

I had found, and it had the lowest rent, to the tune of several hundred dollars! Ironically, my landlords were the best I have ever had. When you take your time and are patient, a little luck will come your way.

I will emphasize that when renting you need to really evaluate your landlords just like they are evaluating you. For most, moving is not a pleasant experience, so my philosophy is why do it more than you have to! When I moved into my new-to-me rental in San Diego, I knew I would be there for at least two years. I ended up being there over four years.

That is another key thing to think about. How long do you plan to live in this place? Can you stay longer, if need be? If you own, will you be able to sell your house in a timely manner, or will you have to try and turn your former home into a rental?

In my situation, I was unsure how long I would be there, but I made sure it was something I could do long-term if I needed to. Thankfully, I had thought that through because I ended up being in the cottage rental far longer than I had originally expected.

I know most of you who are married and have children are going, "Yeah, that is no problem for a single guy, but our situation is different." Yes and no. I know families who have reduced their living area by half with no problem at all. Sure, at first, they and their kids had to get used to the new lifestyle, but once they adapted, I never heard one complaint about not having enough space. Again, it is about facing the challenge and not giving in to the sentiment that "it's just too hard."

Simplifying your life comes with challenges, and you have to keep your eye on the prize at the end. More financial stability and less stuff ultimately means more freedom. I'm not saying that minimizing your living space and having more disposable income is the solution to all your life problems. But I can promise you this: it is easier to figure them out without additional self-perpetuated stress.

The Payoff

The Recession was not kind to most of us. I'll be honest, I ended up selling my house for a significant loss, but I had to make a critical choice. Let the house eventually push me into bankruptcy or sacrifice short-term loss for long-term happiness. These were incredibly tough circumstances, but I don't regret what I did for a second. *I want to emphasize this is the decision I made, but I'm not a financial expert. You will have to weigh your own circumstances and determine what is best for you and your family.*

The payoff for me was undeniable. By forcing myself way out of my comfort zone, I found a great rental place for a great price. Now, I know you are asking, "So how big was the cottage?" My new rental place was around 475 square feet (based on my measurements). That's right, I went from 1,700 to 475 square feet, almost a 75 percent reduction in living space!

Do I recommend everyone make such a drastic change? Of course not. Again, it depends on your situation and your comfort levels. I will tell you that I have no regrets and the thought of ever living in a big house again has not once crossed my mind since I made the change.

Now let's get down to the nitty-gritty—so how much did I save? I was able to go down from $3,500 in basic living expenses per month to $1,100 a month. The best part for me was not just saving a lot of money but also not having all the stress of maintaining and paying for a large house. That was priceless.

Another bonus was that I had to sell a lot of stuff because there was no way it was going to fit into the rental cottage. I made close to $10,000 selling all my extra crap on Craigslist, and I sold most of it in forty-eight hours! I can't explain the cleansing effect this had on my psyche and life. After selling all those useless possessions, it felt as if a huge weight had been lifted off my shoulders. I draw the above advice from my real-life experience. As most of you know from my other books, I never give you advice about things I have never done myself.

I have learned that home ownership not only costs you financially, but it can also put you in a situation where you can get stuck. I used my time in the rental place to plot out my next move (which turned out to be my mobile lifestyle and off-the-grid project!) and make sure I was not rushing into anything I would later regret. I know not everything can be planned for, nor does everything always work out perfectly, but I like to give myself the best odds possible to avoid as many pitfalls as I can.

Operation Travel Trailer: Hello, Tiny Living!

As I explained above, this renting period taught me how to downsize; it also bought me time to get my ultimate plan together. By the time I had been renting for about three years, I had purchased my twenty acres for my off-the-grid house project. I was ready for the next step.

I found that while building a house off the grid, a great way to enjoy the property and save money is to live in an RV on the property. Matter of fact, I have learned that this is how most people build an off-the-grid house. For most, because there is no financing for off-the-grid homes, it usually takes three to five years to complete the project. The upside is you usually have no or very little debt when it is done; the downside is you need someplace to live for the duration. For those interested in the off-the-grid lifestyle, I highly recommend you get my book *Going Off The Grid*, as it is a step-by-step how-to book. For me,

I planned to live the mobile and off-the-grid lifestyle, so I now needed to get a travel trailer.

3

Motorized Transportation and Recreational Vehicles: A Brief History

THE IRON HORSE A.K.A. THE MOTORCYCLE

Humans' first stab at mechanical freedom was the motorcycle, a contraption born of inventors and tinkerers putting small motors onto bicycles. In 1885, Gottlieb Daimler is credited with building the first motorcycle. Daimler's first motorcycle had a single-cylinder Otto-cycle engine mounted in the center of the bicycle frame, which became how almost all motorcycles are designed even to this day.

Humans have always craved freedom, so it is no surprise that we are always striving to improve the mechanical modes of transportation in order to gain more and more freedom. The motorcycle was no exception. It was an incredible invention for the time, but it has three major problems:

1. You can't go very far.

2. You are exposed to the elements.

3. You can't carry very many belongings or personal items.

THE AUTOMOBILE EQUALS FREEDOM (MAYBE)

Prior to the Model T being introduced in 1908 and the Ford Motor Company's assembly line, created in 1913, humans' primary forms of transportation were their feet, large domestic animals, and bicycles. Sure they gave us mobility, but the distance we could cover was limited because they all rely on animals or humans for power. With the advent of the motorized vehicle and the creation of the assembly line, the average person could afford an automobile and travel far greater distances than ever before.

There is some irony, though, to the story of Henry Ford introducing the assembly line. Yes, the affordability of the automobile gave a great deal more freedom to people, but it also inhibited us from having the time to enjoy this newfound freedom by creating what we know today as the "modern work week." Through a lot of trial and error, Henry Ford figured out how long he could work someone doing repetitive tasks and pay them just enough to survive before they would snap or just walk off the job. I guess that automobile-and-freedom thing didn't quite work out how we expected. The irony is that, through the years, ownership of an automobile has represented true freedom all over the globe.

With the industrial revolution, the advent of the assembly line, and the invention of the automobile, Americans migrated from the more rural parts of the country to concentrate in big cities where the jobs were more plentiful. This was a huge shift in the way Americans lived. Free time was becoming harder and harder to find. This lack of leisure time has accelerated so dramatically that many people are considered burned out in today's society.

CAR TWEAKERS CREATE THE FIRST RECREATIONAL VEHICLE

As we learned earlier with the first motorcycle, humans love to tinker and invent. Almost as soon as the first affordable automobiles came off the assembly line, automobile owners began to make alterations to their cars for camping. Because of this, it wasn't long before the first recreational vehicle (RV) was made.

The first official RV was the Pierce-Arrow Touring Landau, and it was introduced at Madison Square Garden in 1910. The Pierce-Arrow came with a back seat that folded into a bed, a sink, and chamber pot toilet that folded down from the back of the seat of the chauffeur. Yep, a chauffeur. So as you can imagine, this Model T of RVs was primarily marketed to the affluent. It didn't take long for other companies to jump on the bandwagon, and before we knew it, the RV was being produced in large numbers. Jump forward to today and the modern RV can almost be had by all. They contain all the modern amenities of today's suburban home, such as an oven, stovetop, microwave, full bathroom, full-size beds, satellite television . . . and so much more.

Now before we just jump right into the different types of RVs, and which one is the best for your lifestyle and goals, we need to get a few things out of the way:

1. You will have to downsize, yes, that means getting rid of a lot of additional crap!

2. You need a plan.

3. Money—this stuff doesn't fall out of the sky.

In the next couple of chapters I will outline what I believe you need to do not only to start living a mobile lifestyle but also to be successful and enjoy it to its fullest.

The Mobile Journey Begins—
My First Travel Trailer

MASS CONFUSION, SO MANY OPTIONS

After purchasing twenty acres for my off-the-grid house, my search for other information started on the dummynet! The internet is good and bad: just as there is a lot of good information, there is also a lot of really bad information. Not only that, but when looking for product information it can be completely overwhelming. I recommend using the internet as a cursory search tool, but doing the majority of your research in person. Yes, that means investing in personal interaction with other human beings!

You can also join social media groups who are living the mobile lifestyle and search posts for the same questions you have. Trust me, you are not the only person who has gone this route. You will be able to ask questions of people who are actually living the lifestyle; it doesn't get any better than that. Again, do not rely on this method solely. You still need to get out and search

THE SIMPLE LIFE GUIDE TO RV LIVING: The Road to Freedom and the Mobile Lifestyle Revolution

for RVs, and after, test out your plan yourself. Like I said earlier, this is your journey, so you need to figure out what is going to work best for you.

I started by looking at various types of RVs, used and new, for sale on the internet. This did not make me an expert by any means, but it did give me insight into the different types, and most importantly, what the heck one of these things cost. I'm not going to candy-coat it—at first, I was completely overwhelmed by the options. Any simple search for RVs for sale will bring up hundreds to thousands of results depending on your search parameters. Patience and due diligence are key. Take your time and do not rush into anything you will regret later.

At that point in my life, I had never owned an RV, so I was a complete rookie. My grandparents had owned an RV that I went on a couple of trips in, and I had several friends who owned them, but that was the extent of my knowledge and experience. Another important point—they were using their RVs for vacations. I was planning on *living* in mine for part of the year, so this was a very different approach to owning an RV.

Once I did my basic research, I contacted a couple of RV dealers and explained to the salespeople what my needs were, the extent of my budget, and how I planned to use the RV. These answers would not address all my questions, but they gave me a starting point to figure out what I was actually looking for and what the price range would be.

I knew that it would be best to purchase a used RV for a couple reasons. First, I had no clue what I was doing, so the lower the investment, the lower the risk. Second, the price would be low enough that I could pay cash and not have to worry about carrying debt, just in case I changed my mind on this lifestyle down the road. There are many people who have bought expensive RVs, used them once, and now the monstrosities sit in their yards while the owners make payments for years for something they never use. Do not be that person!

Here is another option: I didn't do this, but for people who are really not sure about how far they want to go in this mobile lifestyle, or even if it is for them, renting an RV from time to time to test it out is not a bad idea. Here are some of the benefits of doing it this way:

1. The financial commitment is minimal.

2. You can test a variety of options before you purchase.

3. You can evaluate the mobile lifestyle and decide if it's for you.

In addition, if you're interested in living an off-the-grid lifestyle, an RV is a good way to get familiar with its many facets, including camping out in the woods or in remote areas.

Eventually I narrowed down what I was looking for: a travel trailer between eighteen and twenty feet in length. This is considered a small travel trailer by today's standards. The reason I decided to select this size was for two major reasons: First, I had a small truck, so I needed something small and light in order to be able to tow it. Second, a smaller RV meant a lower price of entry to get started.

I ended up purchasing a used eighteen-foot travel trailer from an RV dealer. The reason I ended up purchasing from a dealer was that it came with a warranty. Unless you purchase a very new RV from a private seller, you get what you get. I will tell you, when things break in an RV, it can be an expensive fix unless you are handy and know how to do it yourself. For me, it was worth a little extra money to have that peace of mind that if anything went wrong, the dealer would fix it.

Here was my setup at this point: 2005 4X4 V6 Toyota Tacoma, plus a 2003 eighteen-foot (lightweight—more on this later) tow-behind travel trailer.

Don't worry, I'll explain many of the different options of RV travel and what the descriptions mean in the next chapter. I bought both the truck and travel trailer used. The truck was $22,000, and the travel trailer was $9,000, so a total investment of $31,000

I know some of you are falling out of your chairs thinking that is expensive and completely out of your financial means. As I said earlier, this lifestyle doesn't fall out of trees. You need to have money to get started. Another important point—this was my transportation and home all in one! When you look at it from that perspective, that is dirt cheap.

Also, I made sure this was within my financial means. I paid cash and had no residual payments. I'm a realist. I understand this may not be within your financial grasp, but you can do this cheaper. I'm just giving you this as an example of how I did it. I would say, though, from my experience, this amount is not out of the norm for what people would spend to outfit such a venture. Some people spend far, far more than this because they have the money to do so.

When you factor in that the average sale price of an existing American home in 2018 is $247,000 and new construction with land is $400,000, I consider $31,000 for complete freedom a deal!

RV Classifications

IF YOU DREAM IT, THEY MAKE IT

Now to the nitty-gritty—the different classifications of RVs. When it comes to the classification of RVs, this is where most people have the most confusion and the most questions. There are five major classifications of RVs:

1. Class A

2. Class B

3. Class C

4. Travel Trailer

5. Fifth Wheel

There are even more subclassifications of the above, but to keep it simple, these are the five primary categories you will run into during your search. I'm sure some of you are saying, "What about truck campers," which are campers that fit into the bed of a truck. Can you live a mobile lifestyle with a truck camper? Sure, but I have never met someone doing it because it just isn't practical. For that reason, I have chosen to leave that category off the list. Truck campers are primarily used for camping, fishing, and hunting.

In the descriptions below, I will include what I consider to be the most common size and cost for new RVs in the mobile lifestyle. I could go into the weeds outlining new, used, all the specific sizes, floor plans, etc., but it would just prove confusing. For that detailed information, you have to dedicate yourself to some good old-fashioned work and research.

There is no perfect classification for any one person or lifestyle. The class of RV you choose will depend on several factors such as:

- Budget

- Location

- Lifestyle

- Size of family

- Amenities required

- Size of towing vehicle

- Self-driving RV versus towed RVs

Before I get started, I need to explain one thing: Most RVs today come with "sliders" or "pop-outs." These are expandable units that actually slide out from the RV. These are of great benefit because they can give you a lot of extra room when they are expanded. The downside is that extra room means more money. Pop-outs don't come free. Nonetheless, I would highly recommend getting an RV with one or more slider(s). I have owned RVs with and without sliders, and I will never own one without sliders again.

Class A RV

Let's start with the big daddy, the Class A RV, sometimes referred to as a motor home. These are usually completely self-contained, meaning they have everything a normal house would have, including a power generator for electricity. These are usually thirty to forty feet long and cost between $100,000 and $500,000 new. Some can go for over a million. A perfect example is what you see people using at large sporting events when tailgating or what famous music bands use when touring.

The Good:

- Extraordinarily well-outfitted

- Lots of storage

- Big floor plans with sliders for additional room

- No towing necessary

- You get to pretend you are a rock star!

The Not So Good:

- Expensive

- Terrible gas mileage

- Big—sometimes *really* big

- Can cause high-pucker factor when driving

- Often the most expensive of all RVs to maintain

- Usually requires a mechanic who specializes in Class A RVs

- Special class of driver's license required

- People may think you are a rock star and ask you for your autograph

Class B RV

These are what we called conversion vans when I was growing up. Think of a cargo van converted into an RV. Even though these bad boys are small today, they come with a big price tag, usually in the $75,000 to $125,000 realm. They are usually in the twenty-foot range in length.

The Good:

- Convenient

- No tow vehicle required

- Small and easy to store

- Decent gas mileage

- Easy to maintain

- Suitable for normal parking spaces

- No special driver's license required for operation

The Not So Good:

- Smallest of all RVs

- Usually doesn't come with pop-outs

- Most expensive when comparing size to price

- No rock star bedroom

- Cramped for two people

- Almost no storage

- You will wish you had more space

Class C RV

Of all the RVs, this is the one most people are familiar with. This is what most people rent or use for that summer camping getaway or cross-country trip. I consider this the go-between of the Class A and B RVs. It is a little confusing because you would think this would be called the Class B, and the Class B would be called the Class C. Hey, I just report the facts; maybe someone in the federal government named them! The price range is pretty close to that of the Class Bs, but these will go from the mid-twenties to low-thirties in length, so they're definitely bigger than the Class B.

The Good:

- Bigger than Class B

- Better gas mileage than Class A

- Has some storage

- No special driver's license required

- Does not require a tow vehicle

- Not as expensive as Class A to service

The Not So Good:

- Usually not convenient for long-term living

- Does not usually fit in normal parking spaces

- Poor gas mileage

- Most unstable to drive, as compared to Class A and B

- At most, usually only one pop-out

Travel Trailers

Travel trailers are probably the most common RVs used by people living a mobile lifestyle. People often confuse travel trailers and fifth-wheels. Even though they look similar, trust me these are very different animals in the RV arena. Travel trailers are often described as tow-behinds in order to differentiate them from fifth-wheels because you tow them behind your vehicle using your factory tow hitch receiver. I will describe the fifth-wheel differences in the next section.

Travel trailers are the RV with which I'm most familiar. I have owned three of them, and I'm actually looking to trade up and purchase my fourth in the near future. For me, this was the most practical way to go as it fit my nomadic lifestyle the best. That being said, there are many ways to go in this lifestyle, so don't rule out all the other options. They usually range in the eighteen to thirty-foot range and can cost from $15,000 to $90,000 new.

One More Option: Lightweight or Ultra-Lite Travel Trailers

There is one more subclassification of travel trailer I would like to bring up. I have owned two "lightweight" or "ultra-lite" travel trailers. Companies like to come up with different names, but if there is "light" or "lite" in the name, it is almost always referring to the overall weight of the travel trailer. Just like the name indicates, these trailers are lighter when compared to a normal travel trailer. These lightweight trailers have become more popular recently, as they are primarily designed to be towed by V6 SUVs or light trucks.

The upside is they are smaller and lighter; the downside is they can be pretty pricey and not necessarily designed for long-term living. I would categorize these as ideal RVs for families who are looking to go camping a couple of times per year, who don't want to invest more money in a larger truck, and who have limited space to store a trailer. These are great trailers for people who want to explore but live in a more urban area. They are also great for people looking to test out the more mobile lifestyle, as they are easy to find and rent, and you don't need a special vehicle to tow them.

They usually cost in the range of $12,000 to $25,000.

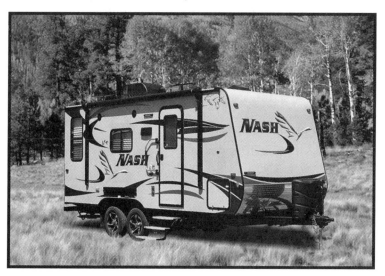

The Good:

- A huge variety from which to choose

- Come in lighter weight versions that can be towed with a V6 vehicle

- Have most of the amenities of Class A trailers at a fraction of the cost

- Can be detached and left, thus freeing tow vehicle for daily use

- Low operating costs

- No engine, so if repairs are needed you aren't stuck

- No special driver's license required

The Not So Good:

- Tricky to maneuver via towing

- Larger vehicles required to tow larger trailers

- Takes time getting used to, especially if you have never towed anything before

- More time setting up and breaking down

- Need a separate generator to operate all electronics when no plug-in utilities available

Fifth-Wheels

OK, this is where it gets tricky for beginners—whether to get a travel trailer or a fifth-wheel. There are two primary differences when it comes to these RVs: size and how they are towed.

As described above, travel trailers tow behind your vehicle usually using the factory tow receiver. A fifth-wheel uses a special receiver that is mounted in the bed of a truck over the rear axle. So instead of hitching it behind the vehicle, you hitch it into the bed of the truck. Because fifth-wheel trailers are attached to the receiver in the bed of your truck, they are better balanced and tow more easily. In addition, as the receiver is in the bed of your truck, the overall length of your fifth-wheeler and tow vehicle is reduced when compared to a tow-behind travel trailer.

People who live long-term in areas and have a family usually prefer fifth-wheels because of their size and amenities. They usually range from thirty to forty feet in length. They are also much higher than a standard travel trailer, so the headroom is similar to a house. The additional size raises their cost to the $50,000 to $100,000 range.

Don't fret, I'll get into greater detail on these two different RVs later in this book.

The Good:

- Not motorized so can detach tow vehicle for daily use

- Much more space than a standard travel trailer

- Amenities are closer to a standard house, like a Class A RV

- Built more for families or larger groups of people

- No engine, so not stranded if it breaks down

- No special driver's license required

The Not So Good:

- Usually much larger than a travel trailer so harder to park and store

- More expensive to maintain than a travel trailer

- Requires a larger vehicle to tow—trucks only

- Cannot be towed by anything but a truck

- Special receiver required, so additional cost

- Receiver is in the back of truck bed, restricting regular use of bed

- Usually cost more than a travel trailer

The Most Common RVs in this Lifestyle

The above sections were to give you a general idea of the different types of RVs. This is by no means an all-encompassing description of each. In order to determine what will work for you, you have to look at them in person. There are so many factors that are directly related to your goals and lifestyle, it would be impossible for me to cover them all. I would definitely recommend looking at each type of RV to become familiar with them before you purchase.

The majority of the RV types I will cover will be the travel trailer and fifth-wheel, as these are the most affordable and popular in the mobile lifestyle. That's not to say that there aren't a lot of people using the other options, but these are the two most common options I have encountered during my years living the lifestyle.

When it comes to what type of person chooses a fifth-wheel or a travel trailer, the pattern I have seen first-hand is this:

Fifth-Wheels – Mostly families choose this option.

Travel Trailers – Mostly single or married couples without children choose this option.

But again, this is not set in stone but a general observation. Just as I usually see older retired people choose Class A motorhomes, because they usually have more financial means to do so.

One last note when it comes to larger fifth-wheels: In the past, no matter what the size of the fifth-wheel, just a standard driver's license was required. While doing my research, one of my friends mentioned that California had recently changed the driver's license requirements. Here are the new requirements for larger fifth-wheels and travel trailers, per the California Department of Motor Vehicles' website:

> *A driver must have a fifth-wheel recreational trailer endorsement added to his/her Class C driver license to pull a fifth-wheel recreational trailer over 10,000 lbs., but not over 15,000 lbs. GVWR, which is not used for hire. This endorsement is not required if the driver has a commercial or noncommercial Class A driver license.*

The reason I bring this up is, as fifth-wheels get bigger and contain more and more creature comforts, other states may follow California.

6

The Tiny House Movement— Is It a Viable Option?

As I write this, the tiny home movement is in full swing. There are numerous TV shows, magazines, and websites dedicated to living the tiny home lifestyle.

So what is a tiny home? It's a house that's constructed on a rolling chassis (like a travel trailer—see picture on the next page) or a permanent home that is 500 square feet or less in size. Obviously, I will be focusing on the tow-behind mobile version, but I think it's important to discuss both because there is a ton of confusion on what a tiny home really is.

These smaller travel-trailer-type tiny homes are really popular with the younger crowd at the moment, but to be honest, I'm not a big fan of these for several reasons that I will outline in this chapter. However, if a tiny home is the choice for you, I don't mean to discourage you from this route.

TINY HOUSE CONSTRUCTION

The base upon which mobile tiny homes are constructed—the aforementioned moveable chassis—is basically a steel frame with wheels, pretty much like a utility trailer that you would tow behind your vehicle. People either purchase plans that show them how to build the structure on this rolling chassis and do it themselves, or they pay a company to build the house to their specifications.

Tiny homes are primarily built with standard wood framing/stick construction, like a typical wooden framed-in house you might see built on a plot of land. Although with mobile tiny homes, the house is built on top of the moveable chassis. These types of tiny homes are usually under eight and a half feet wide and vary in length from twelve to twenty-four feet. They are restricted to thirteen and a half feet in height in order to fit under highway underpasses when being moved.

Why You Shouldn't Jump on This Trend

The primary reason these tiny homes are popular is that they are mobile like a travel trailer, but cheaper than a standard home. Just like anything trendy, there is usually a lot of smoke without a lot of real substance behind the claims. In my view, mobile tiny homes are usually a horrible solution for off-gridders, mobile, and simplified living enthusiasts. Here's why:

- They are trendy, and anything trendy is usually a scam.

- They are actually incredibly expensive, with prices that frequently range from $450 to $650 per square foot (pre-built). In comparison, an average travel trailer will be a third to half this cost.

- They have to be inspected and registered by your local motor vehicle division, meaning you must pay ongoing yearly registration costs.

- A tiny home will typically have higher insurance premiums than an RV.

- They are very heavy, usually over 10,000 pounds. In comparison, my traditional travel trailer weighs a little over 4,000 pounds.

- They can be dangerous to move, because they tend to be very top-heavy.

- They usually lack plumbing; if you want standard RV-style plumbing, it usually comes with an upcharge.

- They are usually made primarily of wood, and are thus a fire hazard when compared to RVs.

- When compared to a fifth-wheel, the fifth-wheel will be bigger, have a nicer interior, be much easier to tow, and cost less.

I'm honestly puzzled by the mobile tiny home movement. RVs have been around for decades, and today are incredibly comfortable, at a fraction of the cost of a tiny home.

I went to one of the more popular mobile tiny home manufacturer websites and priced out one that was around the same size as my current travel trailer. It came out to $70,550. I have seen them go for $100,000 or more! I purchased my second travel trailer brand new for $16,900. Don't get me wrong, the tiny home trailer was made from nicer materials, but it had no more functionality than my travel trailer.

I can't wait until all these people who purchased these mobile tiny homes decide they are done with the trend and try to sell them. I'm fairly certain they are going to lose a ton of money, and that is if anyone is even willing to purchase one of these overpriced sheds on wheels.

OK, I know you are thinking, *Wow, Gary. Talk about putting on the negative hat!* Well, if you are new to my books or my writings, you will learn I do not candy-coat anything. I find a preconstructed tiny home to be a complete waste of money. Not to mention, you are now exposing yourself to a contractor(s). Please see my *Going Off The Grid* book for an entire chapter dedicated to dealing with general contractors. I would highly recommend not dealing with a general contractor unless absolutely necessary, not only to save money but also the pain and stress usually associated with it.

When a Mobile Tiny Home Is a Good Idea

Now on a positive note, if you are fairly handy and possibly looking for a challenge, constructing your own tiny home is not a bad idea. You will be able to do it on your schedule, as well as budget, and build it exactly how you want. From the discussions I have had with people building their own mobile tiny homes, it usually takes from two to six months to complete, and they cost in the $15,000 to $20,000 range. As you know from my off-the-grid adventures, I'm a big fan of the DIY lifestyle, and this would be a great opportunity if you are interested in really testing your skills.

The upside to a tiny home is if you *do* plan to take it up a notch and live off-the-grid, you already have a temporary home or a guesthouse down the road if you ever choose to build a bigger dwelling.

I do want to add something: During my years of living a mobile lifestyle, I have yet to see a tiny home being towed around from place to place. The main reason is I have not found an RV park that accepts tiny homes. Another reason is that these bad boys are dangerous to tow, especially when compared to a fifth-wheel or travel trailer.

So my final thought is a tiny home is really not a viable option for living the mobile lifestyle, as there are much better options available in the RV world that are ready to go. Remember, traditional RVs manufacturers already have over a hundred years of experience. But, I did feel it was necessary to cover the tiny home topic, as I get a ton of questions about them.

As you can see, for the rookie, this mobile lifestyle stuff can be a little confusing in the beginning, so why make it even more so by throwing tiny homes in the mix? For almost all interested in this lifestyle, I would stick to the five major categories of RVs. You'll spend less money, suffer less pain, and can buy it and drive it away in the same day.

7

My Recommended
Equipment for Your RV

After spending years living in an RV, owning several with different options, and looking at probably close to a hundred different RVs in person, there is a definite list of must-haves I would recommend. When you first start on this adventure, you will find so many options, it may be rather daunting. I know in the beginning I made some big mistakes with the first two travel trailers I purchased. Not that they were bad travel trailers—the truth was I just didn't know or understand what options I would need to live the mobile lifestyle. Now, not all these options will be necessary for you, but understanding all or most of them will definitely not be a mistake. You can choose which you want to include and which are unnecessary. I'm pretty confident they will get used or have a benefit at some point in your journey.

ALL-SEASONS/ALL-CONDITIONS CLASSIFICATION

This was probably the biggest mistake I made in the beginning. As a matter of fact, I didn't even know that the "all seasons" classification existed and what it meant until after I purchased my second travel trailer.

Basically, this is an RV that has upgraded insulation value in its walls and ceiling. In some cases, this could also mean an upgrade in windows (more on this later). Trust me, once I bought my first all-season classified travel trailer, there was no way I would go back. Yes, it made that big of a difference! An RV without this classification is usually considered a casual camper RV. These are what people get who go camping a couple of times per year in nicer weather. These types of RVs can be quite a bit cheaper than an all-season rated one.

From firsthand experience, I will tell you that if you live or spend prolonged periods of time in a casual camper RV (one without all-season features), you will cook in the summer and freeze in the winter. Your air conditioner and heater will be running nonstop, and during the more severe weather, neither will likely be able to keep up with the conditions

You might ask why this would be a big deal when you are plugged into utilities at an RV park. Depending where you are, a lot of RV parks will charge you separately for electricity. One last point of importance is that I have found the construction of all-season rated RVs far superior to their non-rated counterparts.

So how will you know a particular RV is rated for all seasons? It will have a fairly obvious sticker right next to the front door indicating this. Also in the list of features/options, there will be a line item indicating the wall and ceiling insulation values (see below example, as taken from my current travel trailer):

All-Conditions / Four-Season Insulation With R-14
Ceiling R-15 Reflective Foil Insulation in Roof / Slide

The higher the "R" rating of insulation, the better insulated it will be. For example, R-16 is a better insulation value than R-14.

Also make sure the slides/pop-outs have the same insulation as the walls. My second travel trailer had very little insulation in the slide, and it was an absolute nightmare. It had a closet in the slide that would fill with condensation during the winter because of the big temperature difference between the outside and the inside.

OFF-ROAD CHASSIS

Having an off-road chassis (the framework on which your RV is built) will be of great benefit when taking your RV to a remote location. An off-road chassis is built to withstand rougher road conditions and will have more ground clearance and heavy-duty suspension.

Some of you might be wondering why you should care about an off-road chassis. If you plan to live more remotely and/or use your RV for a permanent or temporary dwelling, this will be critical. Most RVs do not come with this option. However, even if you just plan to use your RV for occasional camping, hunting, or fishing trips in more remote areas, I would still heavily recommend this option. There is nothing worse than bottoming out, dragging parts of your RV, or getting stuck in tougher road conditions. Not to mention, possibly ruining your RV or severely damaging it. Trust me, I have done it, and it is not a pleasant experience.

THERMAL PANE/DUAL PANE WINDOWS

Just like the all-season option this is another biggie! My first two travel trailers had single-pane windows (meaning a single piece of glass). During rainy days or during the winter, they continuously fogged up with condensation. So much so, that the condensation would drip down the wall *inside* the trailer at times . . . not good. Not only that, I could hear everything through them when they were shut.

Just like your house's windows, thermal/dual-pane windows are two pieces of glass with gas injected between them. This means they possess a much better insulation value, exhibit less fogging/condensation, and insulate better against outdoor noise. They're also harder to break for that deadbeat thief. The downside is they are much more expensive, but they're worth every penny. I would never own an RV without them.

TEN-GALLON GAS/ELECTRIC QUICK-RECOVERY WATER HEATER

OK, like the off-road chassis, you are probably wondering why this would be a big deal. Well, my first two travel trailers had six-gallon gas-only water heaters, and all I can say is they suck. They are fine for that occasional camping trip, but that's it. There is pretty much no way more than one person is going to be able to take a shower with a six-gallon water heater.

Gas-only means you have to turn them on when hot water is needed; if you run them continuously, you will drain your propane gas tanks very quickly. So this means you need to turn the water heater on a good fifteen minutes before you take a shower or need hot water to wash dishes. When you throw in the fact that you will forget to turn off the gas draining your propane tank, a six-gallon water tank is just a pain in the butt to deal with.

There is no comparison when you have an RV with a ten-gallon gas/electric water heater. First, two people can take showers back-to-back—not long showers, but it's at least possible with this option. The electric option means that when it's plugged in to a utility-tied RV hookup, you can have the water heater on continuously just like a normal house's water heater. The downside is you may have to pay for the extra electricity if the RV park charges for it, but I will guarantee it will be cheaper than paying for the propane in the gas-only option.

Not to say the gas option is bad, it's just way better to have both. The electric option means you can have continuous hot water; the gas is for dry camping (more on this later) and can be used when you need hot water fast—it heats the water tank quicker than the electric option. An example would be when you first hook up your RV at a location and want to use hot water right away; you'd use the gas option until water is hot, then you can switch to the electric option.

THIRTY-GALLON OR ABOVE DUAL PROPANE STORAGE TANKS

This is another feature that you might think would not be a big deal, but it is critical to your comfort and ease of operation of gas appliances. These are the items inside your RV that run off your propane tanks:

• Stove

• Oven

• Heater

• Water Heater

• Optional BBQ Line

Why are dual tanks so important? If you have only one tank, when it goes empty you are stuck. With two tanks, once one runs out you can quickly switch over to the full tank and continue what you were doing. There is nothing worse than cooking dinner and running out of propane when you only have one tank. Not to mention, if you are not close to a place that can refill tanks immediately it is going to be even a bigger pain in the you-know-what.

I have had the standard fifteen- to twenty-gallon propane tanks, and I will never go back to these smaller devices. Just like the comparison between the six-gallon water heater as compared to the ten-gallon water heater, there is a huge difference when it comes to operation time. When plugged into RV hookup utilities, I have gone several months without filling up my thirty-gallon propane tanks.

Some people who live, or travel for lengthy periods, in their RVs will actually purchase bigger than thirty-gallon propane tanks. For me, I just haven't found it necessary at this point, but if you are going without access to electricity for an extended period, bigger tanks could be a big deal.

HEATED STORAGE TANKS

Your RV will come with storage tanks for water, gray water, and black water. Your water tank is for water you want to use for sink faucets, toilets, and showers. This is stored water when you do not have access to water hookups, such as those provided at a standard RV park. Gray water is the used water that comes from your sinks and shower. This water is stored in an internal tank when you do not have access to sewage hookups. Your black water is the sewage from your toilet. The gray and black water waste have separate storage tanks contained in your RV.

I'm sure you can quickly see the importance of having heated storage tanks if you are staying/living in an area that dips below freezing temperatures. If your black water contents freeze, you are in deep doo-doo. Yes, pun intended.

EXTERIOR SHOWER

Of all the above, this seems to be the least critical, but when I have not had it I have missed it. I have found it to be pretty critical in remote locations. Because the exterior shower is hooked up to the hot water tank, you can clean various things like greasy BBQ grills/components; wild game or fish utility utensils; stinky, dirty pets; and, of course, yourself. I purchased my second travel trailer without an external shower, and as in the past, I learned I will never do without this option again.

For the seasoned RV individual some of these features are pretty obvious, but for the newbie it is easy not to know about the importance of some options, like an external shower. Now these options are not always included in your RV purchase, but I have found them to be the most important for the mobile RV lifestyle. With that said, I will leave you with one other option that you do not need to get from a dealer or have included with your RV.

POWER GENERATOR

In your more expensive RVs, a pre-installed power generator will come standard, but most RVs that are in most people's price range will not come with a generator. I have found they are not commonly offered in travel trailers, but they are an upgrade option. They are more commonly found in your Class A and Fifth-Wheel RVs due to their size and how they are used.

Dry Camping Defined

This is probably a good place to discuss "dry camping" as this directly relates to using a generator. When you go to purchase an RV from a dealer, you will more than likely hear the term dry camping being thrown around. Dry camping refers to not having any access to external RV hookups for power, water, and sewage. When dry camping, you will rely on your gray and black water storage tanks. Unless you have a mobile, and fairly powerful, solar power system, you will have to rely on your RV storage batteries for power. RV storage batteries will not run anything on the AC power side, as they are DC only. Also they provide a short-term power supply solution only, primarily able to run your interior/exterior RV lights.

In order to run all your equipment and accessories in your RV while dry camping, you will need to use a generator. Now if you are going to use your RV as a temporary or permanent living situation on a remote piece of land, you can put in your own septic, well, and power systems. Again, this all depends on what your goals and your living desires are.

I will not be going into how to set up a separate sewage, power, and water system on a remote piece of land because this is covered in *Going Off The Grid* in great detail.

Why Would You Need a Generator?

An important point to clarify on how your RV electrical system works is that when not plugged into an external power source, your RV components will run off DC power just like your automobile. Without getting into the weeds, your home runs on AC power, which is the standard, so almost all household appliances and electrical items run off this type of power. If you want to go into geek-land, there are numerous articles on the internet explaining the difference between AC and DC power.

When not plugged into an external power source, your RV power outlets will not work, you cannot run your air conditioner, microwave, electric water heater, or anything else that requires AC power. Your refrigerator and heater will still work, as they are also powered by DC 12-volt power and by propane (RV refrigerators run on AC electricity or propane.)

In order to run these above items when not hooked up to external power, you will need a generator. You can get one installed if your RV does not have one already hardwired into the electrical system, or you can carry a portable one.

The benefits of having either a hardwired or portable generator are pretty obvious: no matter what the situation, you can run everything. Without a generator, when not hooked up to an outside power source, you will only be able to run some items. So if you end up staying in places that do not have a power source, a generator is pretty essential.

What Type and Size of Generator Do You Need?

The equipment your RV comes with will dictate the type and size of generator you select. Again, without going into Neverland, there are a ton of generator options. I will stick to the most common types to make it easy, as these choices will fill the requirements for most.

Most Class A motor homes come self-contained, meaning they already have a generator hardwired into their electrical system. If your Class A doesn't have a hardwired generator, it can get a little tricky. Class As, due to their bigger size, will usually be outfitted with larger and more energy-sucking appliances. What does this mean? The generator required to run all those appliances will probably have to be a minimum of 5,000 watts (or 5kW for kilowatts). A typical off-the-shelf portable 5k generator is going to be pretty heavy, so the odds of you toting one of these around is pretty slim. Again that is why Class As have large price tags: they become equipped with pretty much everything.

Your Class B and C motor homes usually do not come with a hardwired generator as a standard option, but you can opt to have one installed. The same option usually goes for fifth-wheels and travel trailers. Fifth-wheels again, due to the higher price and size, will more often come with a hardwired generator as a standard option.

For most of the remaining RVs outside of the fifth-wheel and Class A classifications, you can get away with a smaller portable generator. Nonetheless, today's modern RV in the smaller classification can still be an energy hog. Per my personal experience and talking with numerous RV dealers and parts centers, the minimum I would recommend you buy to run everything in your modern, smaller RV would be a 3,000-watt/3-kW generator.

Here's the catch: Even a portable 3kW generator is pretty heavy . . . in the 100-pound range. Most do come with handles and wheels, but they are still pretty difficult to move around. I have a 3100-watt generator and I have to be strategic about where I load it, so I can get it in a place where I can use it without killing or hurting myself.

Another option I have seen is to daisy-chain/wire two or three smaller generators together in order to be able to maneuver them easier.

In addition, the new generators are coming RV-ready, which means you don't need any special power plug adapters from your RV to the generator. It has been very common in the past to have to get adapters to be able to plug your RV's power plug into a portable generator. You will have to determine which power plug your RV has in order to purchase the right generator that will work without an adapter.

You are probably saying, *Whew, this is pretty complicated stuff.* It can be, depending on whether you want to have a generator as a backup or to use when you have no access to standard RV hookups.

If you never plan to live remotely or dry camp, but you *do* plan to live in RV parks with utility hookups, a generator is probably not that important. If you decide that you want a portable generator, they usually go for $700 to $2,000. To have one permanently installed will cost more, but the price will depend on the size and installation location. I have looked into this option, and it just wasn't cost effective. My current 3,100-watt portable generator cost $700.

RV Basics—Tips to Make Your Life Easier

Oh, if I only knew then what I know now! When I first started, I had absolutely no clue what I was doing. A lot of lessons were learned by trial and error. I think these simple tips will definitely make your life a lot easier, especially in the beginning.

THE STINKY SLINKY—A SNAKE YOU DON'T WANT TO MESS WITH

Probably one of the most confusing things in the beginning is how to use your gray and black water clean-out system. Your RV clean-out system is reminiscent of a house's plumbing system. It empties the water and sewage out of your RV. Some RVs will have two clean-out systems for the gray water (sinks and shower). The reason for this is if the kitchen and bathroom are in two different parts of your RV, there may not be adequate slope for the gray water to drain properly with just one drain system.

What is the Stinky Slinky?

If you talk to anyone who has been living the RV life, the one thing we all agree on is we hate using what we call the "stinky slinky!" The stinky slinky is the term used for the slinky-like expandable hose that goes from your RV clean-out to the sewer system located at the place where you are staying. Yep, as you have already probably determined the stinky slinky gets its name from looking like a slinky and stinking from all of the sewage that goes through it. I'll put this nicely: since the expandable pipe has ridges in it, your poo and other disgusting things will get caught in valleys.

There is no getting around the stinky slinky; it is a necessary evil.

How to Tame the Stinky Snake

Here is some good advice in order to deal with the stinky slinky:

- Don't go on the cheap; buy the heavy-duty version. Trust me, I bought the cheap off-the-shelf version, and it split because of sun exposure. Yep, poop and pee everywhere, all because I didn't notice the failure until after I'd opened the clean-out valve . . . not a pleasant experience!

- Have at least one extra section of stinky slinky, just in case the above happens.

- If you use the stinky slinky for an extended period of time and move on, I would recommend just tossing it and use a new one at your next location. Yes, you can clean it out, but you risk getting blasted in the face with you-know-what.

- When hooking up the stinky slinky, use disposable latex

gloves. Yep, another lesson I learned after having gotten you-know-what all over my hands and arms.

- Keep the clean-out valve closed until your stinky slinky is completely hooked up.

- This is probably the most important lesson and the one most people get wrong: Keep your black water valve closed until your black water tank is about three-quarters full, then open it to drain into your sewage system. This way you will avoid having sewer smell coming back into your travel trailer. In addition, by storing sewage in tank until it's three-quarters full, it allows contents to dissolve into a liquid, thus avoiding chunks of fun stuff getting stuck in the stinky slinky. Most people just leave both the black and gray water valve open all the time, which does not allow for solids to dissolve; instead, they get stuck in the stinky slinky. You can imagine what the condition the stinky slinky will be in in just a couple weeks . . . not pleasant. Not to mention, you risk having a blockage causing the glorious sewage to overflow inside your trailer.

- Use a bio-dissolving product in the black water tank. This will help assure your solids will liquefy, so they do not get caught in the stinky slinky. There are numerous brands—make sure to sign up for my updates to get my recommended products and reference list.

- Keep the gray water valve open, as this will help keep the stinky slinky clean and wash stinky waste down the sewage line.

- When preparing to dump your black water tank, close and fill your gray water tank to one-half to three-quarters full (just turn on faucet at one sink). After you dump the black water tank, close and then dump the gray water. This helps clean out the stinky slinky after a black water dump.

- Do not leave or walk away from your RV while partially filling up the gray water tank as outlined above. Yes, you guessed it—I have done this to find water pouring out of my RV when I returned. Not to mention, I have seen other people make the same mistake. I usually let it run no longer than ten to fifteen minutes, then check my tank level on the internal monitoring board (RVs come with a monitoring board that tells you how full your tanks are). The best way to avoid overflowing is to set up a timer for ten minutes. Of course, this could change depending on the size of your holding tanks.

- Lastly, the best way to keep your septic and stinky slinky free from trouble and clogs is to use made-for-RV dissolving toilet paper only, and never flush anything besides dissolving toilet paper, poop, and pee down your toilet. Yes, ladies, just like your home system, that means no female care products! If you don't follow the above rules, I will guarantee endless stink and pain when dealing with your septic system.

BEST WATER HOSE FOR RV EXTERIOR USES

Another pain is carrying around hoses for uses outside of your RV. They are heavy, hard to store, and usually leak water all over the place when you store them. OK, I'm not a big "As Seen on TV" product guy, as most of that stuff is complete junk. But, I recently found a great solution for the above problem. Some of you may have seen the adds for the metal-cased water hoses on recent infomercials. They claim they do not kink, will not tear or get cut by sharp objects . . . and I will tell you, they were not bullshitting. I bought one of these hoses to try out on my RV after having yet another rubber hose go bad and start leaking, and I was really surprised.

These hoses are perfect for the RVer. They are way lighter, take up much less space, and so far, mine have not leaked at all. I have two of these that I use for different applications, such as rinsing off my RV or washing my car. There is a downside to these type of hoses, though: they have a narrower diameter, thus less water pressure. Now this is not good for a normal house water hose, but for most tasks while living the RV life I have found this type of hose to be more than good enough to get the job done.

WHY YOU NEED A DRINKING WATER SAFE HOSE

At the time I write this there is no version of the above metal-cased hose that is rated "drinking water safe." What that means is you **do not** want to use the above, or any other hose not rated as drinking water safe, for your internal RV water appliances. The primary reason is that hoses not rated safe for drinking water can leach harmful chemicals into your water.

Over the years I have used various drinking water-rated hoses, and I'll tell you they are pretty lousy in the durability department. Recently I tried yet another one, and so far it has worked pretty well. I've included the name and model number in the resource list I mentioned at the beginning of this book.

In addition, I would recommend using a water filter, either in line with your water hose or on your kitchen sink faucet. I personally never drink the water from my RV water faucets, but that is my preference.

WATER HOOKUP ELBOW

Something as small as a three- or four-dollar part may not seem like a big deal, but you'd be surprised by how these little things can make a big difference. This part can pretty much be found at any place selling RV parts, but I've been surprised by how many people don't use it.

This part is simply a ninety-degree brass fitting from your water hose to your RV exterior water hookup. Why is this part important? It will make your life so much easier as these exterior RV water hookups stick straight out from the side of your RV, putting a lot of pressure on your water hose and RV threaded fitting. So the result is usually a water hookup that leaks. At first it will not leak, but over time, it will get worse and worse. This simple ninety-degree brass fitting takes a great deal of pressure off the RV hookup and water hose fittings. Since I started using this part several years ago, my exterior RV water connection has never leaked when properly tightened.

MAKING SURE YOUR WATER LINES DO NOT FREEZE IN COLD WEATHER

This is a question I have been asked several times by my followers looking to get into the mobile living lifestyle or already actively living it: *How do I avoid my water lines freezing in my RV in the winter?*

There are actually two separate parts to prevent plumbing lines from freezing because you have internal and exterior plumbing in your RV. Unlike a house, your internal water lines and plumbing will not be buried in the ground per the freeze depth, or covered with insulation in your walls. Your RV internal plumbing has some insulation around it, but not enough to stop it from freezing during really cold months. In addition, your external water hookup, in the form of a standard garden hose, will definitely freeze in colder climates. There are some tips below to help you avoid freezing your internal and external plumbing.

When hooked up to exterior power in our RVs, a lot of us like to use space heaters to save on propane gas because that is what the RV heater runs on. The downside to this is you usually cannot generate enough heat throughout the RV to prevent the internal plumbing lines from freezing in more extreme cold weather. To avoid this, you need to run the RV's propane gas-powered heater, as its ducting runs through where most of your internal plumbing lines run, thus keeping them above the freezing point.

When it comes to the external water line hookup, if you are in temperatures that don't dip too much below freezing, insulated hose tubing usually works just fine. If you are in more extreme cold weather, you will need to put a thermal temperature heating line around water hose. These have been around forever; we used them on our water heater's exposed waterlines when I was a kid. They plug into a normal 120v/15-amp outlet that RVs have on the outside for powering external devices. In addition, if you are at a standard RV park, you can plug into their power source at your RV space. They come in various lengths, depending on the length you need for external pipes or your water hose.

You really need to pay attention when you are plugging an external electrical device into your external RV outlet. If it is going to be exposed to severe weather, you are going to have to make sure your outlet is protected against rain or snow getting into it.

Another piece of advice is to place insulation around your external water source (main valve where water is coming from). If you are in a cold-weather environment, you will need to experiment with what works best for you as I have seen many different setups over the years.

If by chance your lines freeze, here are two methods I have used: For internal hoses, turn on your heater and let it run for fifteen minutes, then test it to see if water will flow out of your faucets. If this doesn't work, more than likely your external hose is frozen. Run an extension cord (this only works if you are plugged into electrical power or have a generator) and use a hair dryer to attempt to unfreeze your external water line enough to allow water to flow.

Here is one more piece of advice that many who grew up in cold areas use in their houses during the winter months: Before you go to bed or when freezing weather is present, leave your internal faucets on just enough to have a constant drip. This will keep the water flowing enough to usually prevent freezing.

USING PLASTIC TOTES FOR STORAGE

When living the mobile RV life, plastic totes of various sizes are a must. When moving from place to place, these are the easiest and cheapest ways to store your items. A mistake people often make is to not store items that can move around in their RV while moving from location to location. People find objects scattered from end to end when they stop. I use plastic totes not only to store items when not in use, but also when I pack up to take off. When in travel status, I store all breakable items as well as anything that can shift while the RV is moving.

Quick Tip

For that menace, the "stinky slinky," I recommend getting a plastic tote with a sealable gasket for the lid. Trust me on this, the stinky slinky . . . well, it stinks. Hence, the name! I have stored it in a normal tote to find that wherever I have stored the tote, the area smells like poop.

Yes, the bumpers in RVs have a place to slide and store the stinky slinky, but I have found that this location makes my bumper and the rear of the RV stink. You can wash out the tote, or throw it away if it becomes unusable down the line. You can't do that with your RV bumper.

WEIGHT DISTRIBUTION AND ANTI-SWAY SYSTEM (TRAVEL TRAILERS ONLY)

If you plan to regularly tow a travel trailer, a weight distribution and anti-sway system is an absolute must. They can be a little costly, reaching the $500 to $1,000 price range installed, but they are worth every penny. A weight distribution and anti-sway system is used to stabilize and reduce the stress and weight on the tow-hitch when towing a travel trailer. I have towed travel trailers with and without this system, and there is no comparison. As a matter of fact, I will never tow a travel trailer without one.

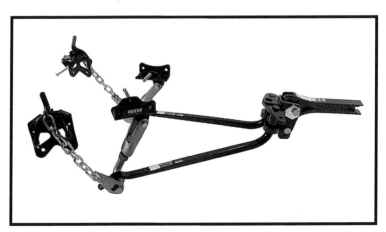

Without one of these systems you can feel every bump and sway of your travel trailer, causing a lot of butt puckering. With an anti-sway system, you can literally forget you are towing anything behind you.

Quick Tip

When using a weight distribution and anti-sway system, make sure to disengage the anti-sway and weight distribution bars when backing the trailer in place to store or park. This will make your life a lot easier as the system is intended for towing and not necessarily for backing up and parking.

Purchasing the Right Tow Vehicle for Fifth-Wheels and Travel Trailers

There is nothing worse than towing a travel trailer or fifth-wheel with an undersized or wrong type of vehicle. Your butt will be puckered tight enough to make diamonds out of coal, and you will need an old school headband to keep the sweat out of your eyes. I'm not over exaggerating the necessity of acquiring the right type and size vehicle for the job—it is critical.

Oh, I know there is a group out there that says it's not a big deal to tow a small travel trailer with a small V6 SUV or car. I will agree if the travel trailer is a small one that only has a bed and some storage, but trust me, you are better off camping in a tent if you intend to live the mobile lifestyle for any length of time. Not only is it dangerous towing a normal-size travel trailer or fifth-wheel with a small car or truck, but it will also wear out that vehicle at a highly accelerated rate. It will also expose you to a greater chance of breakdown and getting stranded due to stress put on the vehicle.

LESSONS LEARNED

Yes, I towed my first travel trailer with a V6 Toyota Tacoma, but not for long. I realized it was not the proper vehicle if I intended to tow my travel trailer long distances. What made me see the light was towing my twelve-foot utility trailer with my Tacoma in a haul from California to Washington. It was painfully obvious this was the wrong truck for the job. While heading up one of my steep switchbacks to my off-the-grid property, my transmission overheated and I got stuck. It took me three hours of unloading the utility trailer and letting the transmission cool, before I could continue on. But I had to break up the items I had into smaller loads to get it to the top of the property and the storage shed.

Not to mention, I got stuck again when my utility trailer drifted off the side of the road, and the ATV I had strapped down broke a strap and almost flipped out of the trailer. I'm a former Navy and law enforcement guy, but I'm sure I broke some records with the curse words that came flying out of my mouth in this situation.

Needless to say, I traded my Tacoma for a half-ton V8 Toyota Tundra a week later. Not only did this allow me to tow my trailer with a vehicle made for towing, but it also allowed me to upgrade the size and weight of my travel trailer as my living requirements changed.

My second generation of mobile living setup was a 2014 Toyota Tundra and a twenty-three-foot travel trailer with a cost of $55,000 for both. This time, I stepped up and bought both the travel trailer and truck new, but you can definitely buy used. I just wanted to have warranties on both because I was at a point where I didn't want to have to deal with any repair issues on my own.

TRUCK SIZE, HAULING WEIGHT CAPACITY, AND TORQUE

The above vehicle and travel trailer combination worked well for the next couple of years. After looking at a lot of other people's setups for living in more rural areas, I came up with my ultimate tow and work vehicle for the job. My goal was to accommodate the combination of off-the-grid living and towing a travel trailer thousands of miles per year.

My final setup has come from years of living a remote and mobile lifestyle. It may not be the perfect setup for you, but I found it to be the best for me. I spent over six months looking at every make and model of truck in the three-quarter to one-ton classification.

Tonnage rating for trucks used to mean specific hauling capacities, but that has changed in recent years. Trucks are usually categorized as light-truck, one-half, three-quarter, and one-ton when it comes to towing and hauling ratings. The important thing to remember is that a light truck is the lowest and one-ton is the highest when it comes to hauling and towing capacity. You will have to look at the specifications of the truck you are interested in to see the true hauling and towing weight rating.

Oh boy, are we having fun yet? I know this is getting a little confusing, but we probably should briefly discuss foot-pounds of torque while we're at it. One of the most important specifications to look at when searching for a tow vehicle is the amount of torque it has. Torque is simply the power transferred from the engine and transmission to the wheels. This is an oversimplification, but it's the best description to use when discussing towing. I'm sure some engineers and gearheads are cussing at my explanation, but again, if you want to get in the weeds, there is a ton of information on what torque means on the internet. Basically, the more torque you have, the more power you will have to tow. You can have a massive engine, but if you can't transfer that engine power (horsepower) into torque, it's a waste of money and gas.

What Is a Dually Truck and Is It Better for Towing?

For those of us who grew up in the sticks, "dually trucks" were and are still pretty common. So what is a dually truck? It is basically a heavy-duty truck that has two wheels on each side of the rear axle.

Are they better for towing? Simply, yes, they are. Here's why: they have heavier duty suspension, transmission, and rear-end and gear ratios than your typical heavy-duty truck. These trucks are designed purely for hauling and towing heavy loads. Do you need one of these in order to live the mobile lifestyle? No, these are primarily used by people who have larger than average fifth-wheel trailers.

The downside to a dually, is they are . . . well, big, which means they don't get good gas mileage, they're expensive, and they're not usually as good off-road as regular 4-wheel-drive heavy-duty trucks.

If you're one of those people who plans to live in a monster-size fifth-wheel instead of building a house on a remote piece of land or using it in between building your off-the-grid house, I would recommend hiring someone with a dually or larger tow vehicle to put it in place on your property. I consider this a cheaper and much safer option than buying an expensive dually that you may not need, or towing yourself with an undersize vehicle.

Gas or Diesel Engine?

Until my latest truck upgrade, which has a diesel-powered engine, I had only owned gas-powered trucks. Now that I've owned a diesel-powered truck I can tell you that it:

- Has more torque than a gas-powered truck, which makes for easier towing

- Runs at lower RPMs, meaning less wear over its lifetime

- Gets better gas mileage, especially when towing

- Has many fewer emission than previous versions

- Tends to be more durable

The downside is that diesel trucks are more expensive, particularly when including maintenance. But, even with the additional cost, I consider a diesel-powered truck to be far superior to a gas-powered truck when living the mobile lifestyle. I will say from experience, people living the mobile lifestyle that are towing and living in trailers are driving diesel-powered trucks at a much higher percentage than those driving gas-powered trucks.

Air Suspension

One last option for those who are looking into getting a larger-size fifth-wheel or travel trailer: Even though heavy-duty trucks come with heaver-duty suspension, with the increasing options and size of today's travel trailers, you may want to upgrade your rear suspension to what is called "air suspension or air bags."

Again, I don't want to go into the various suspension upgrades for trucks, as there are numerous options. Instead, I want to focus on the primary rear suspension upgrade for towing RV trailers.

All automobiles today come with what is called the Gross Vehicle Weight Rating (GVWR). Before you purchase your travel trailer or fifth-wheel, you need to make sure your vehicle towing capability is rated high enough to tow it. As an example, this rating (GVWR), along with your truck's towing capacity, is determined by many factors, including engine size, gear ratio, wheel and tire package, cab and bed configuration, transmission, and axles.

Air suspension systems do not increase your towing capacity; many factors in your GVWR determine this. The most common air suspension system places an airbag and corresponding brackets over the rear axle or leaf spring. So if this doesn't increase the towing capacity of your vehicle, why would we install an air suspension system? Because it's used to reduce rear vehicle sag and permits a smoother and more stable vehicle ride while towing.

MY TOWING TRUCK RECOMMENDATION

OK, I know I went off on a couple of tangents here, but this is important stuff. You can save a lot of money by purchasing the right vehicle out of the gate. Of course, it all depends on budget and how much you are comfortable spending. The towing vehicle I will recommend below is not cheap . . . even used!

Drumroll, please! For those serious about this lifestyle, I recommend a one-ton diesel truck with four-wheel drive. As a matter of fact, I have never been able to figure out why you would ever own a truck without four-wheel drive, but that is a topic for another time.

I would recommend at least a three-quarter ton, but optimal is an one-ton diesel truck with at least 800 pound-foot of torque.

During my long search, which included both three-quarter and one-ton trucks, I finally decided on a new 2016 Dodge RAM 3500 Heavy Duty one-ton turbo diesel. The upside is I can tow just about everything; the downside is these types of rated trucks are not cheap. New, they range from about $55,000 to $70,000 depending on the package and accessories you pick.

Some of you are probably rolling your eyes thinking this lifestyle is a fantasy when you look at the prices I'm throwing out. Remember, this is a journey, and you don't have to spend that type of money to do it. I did this over several years because I needed to figure out what my lifestyle would ultimately be, and most importantly, what I could afford. I know people who have started out dirt cheap, buying used truck and trailers. That being said, I would recommend a beginning budget of at least $35,000 for both a towing vehicle and trailer, if you can swing it.

For some, this might seem impossible, but remember the prices I outlined earlier for the average price of a pre-owned or a new construction home today. The above price is pennies when compared to that.

As with the off-the-grid lifestyle, I say this time and time again . . . nothing comes for free. You need two things to get into this lifestyle: a plan and money. Most people love to live in dreamland and think they can just barter and sell some pelts to live this lifestyle. I'm going to tell you firsthand, money is still how our society operates. It will do so for the foreseeable future. If you can find someone who will take labor and other items in trade, do it. But for most, this lifestyle will require you to save and come up with a viable plan in order to achieve your mobile living dreams.

For less than $100,000, you can have a top-notch tow vehicle and travel trailer, fifth-wheel, or Class A/B/C motorhome brand-new. Yes, that is some serious cash, but that is a small fraction of the interest you will pay owning the average American home with a thirty-year loan. Not to mention, most people who borrow money for college today can easily go over this amount. You just have to put everything into perspective when looking at this lifestyle. To me, the above total is cheap when it comes to living a truly free life the way you want.

I will end this chapter with my current mobile lifestyle setup. At the time I wrote this, I have a 2016 Dodge RAM 3500 one-ton turbo diesel and a Nash twenty-four-foot all-season travel trailer. Total cost is in the neighborhood of $78,000. Both these were purchased brand-new. I do plan to upgrade to a new thirty-foot Arctic Fox all-season travel trailer in the next twelve months. My total will still be under the $100,000 mark which, for the type of lifestyle I live, is a deal!

10

Creature Comforts While Living Mobile

As I have said previously, when it comes to the mobile lifestyle, the sky's the limit. There are products and accessories for pretty much any type of lifestyle you wish to live. Today, I would say most new middle- to upper-end RVs are nicer than a majority of homes. Today's RVs that most people can afford can come with multiple TVs, an electric fireplace, and even a washer and dryer. It seems every time I go looking, there are new accessories coming out for RV living. Below I will focus on some of the accessories I think most people would be interested in.

ACCESS TO HIGH-QUALITY TV CHANNELS

Probably the most popular item is having access to TV stations as you would at home. Even though the technology is not perfect, it has gotten a lot better over the last five years. Satellite TV companies are realizing a lot more people are traveling in RVs, and they want access to quality TV channels. Not long ago, the equipment to obtain this was bulky, expensive, and had a lot of limitations.

Today, you can pretty much get HD-quality TV with DVR capabilities if you are willing to spend the money. I will say, though, even with recent advances in technology, you cannot use the high-end satellite receivers that record up to sixteen channels at one time like you can with a large DVR at home. OK, actually you can, but I will explain how it is a big pain to do this with today's RV satellite equipment. There are two main manufacturers of RV mobile satellite equipment. They are:

- Winegard

- King

Full disclosure: At the time I'm writing this, I have only used Winegard products, but I have seen both types of mobile satellites during my years of travel. It is important to understand these are mobile satellites only. This does not include the channel packages and satellite receivers from Dish Network or Direct TV.

These systems will automatically point the mobile satellite dish and acquire the satellite signal. There are multiple versions depending on how many TVs you have, whether you get HD or SD picture quality, and if you want the satellite to be completely mobile or mounted to your RV. The price range of these mobile satellites, minus satellite receivers and channel subscriptions, spans from $300 to $1,500.

For those who want to use their high-end home satellite equipment while on the road, first know that Dish Network and Direct TV flat-out do not want you to do this. Their high-end receivers are more easily damaged when bumped and/or jarred. Per my understanding, they will probably not cover any damage to these high-end satellite home receivers (if you lease the receivers from them) if you damage them while in use in your RV. At this time, the only way you can use these high-end home receivers is to use a tripod with your home satellite dish attached. This means you must manually point your satellite dish in order to acquire the signal.

I have used the tripod method for the last couple years, and I would not recommend it. In fact, I have purchased an RV mobile system from Winegard because other options are just too much of a pain. It is not easy to manually find the satellite signal using this system. Sure, I have done it, but usually with a bunch of colorful words being muttered during the process.

Another option is accessing your home TV channels that satellite and cable TV companies have started to provide via the internet. For this to work you must have reliable home internet service, as it runs off of your home internet router. The downside is you have to watch it on your tablet, phone, or laptop. I have not gotten a straight answer to the question of whether an internet-ready TV will circumvent the above, but I'm sure it's only a matter of time before this happens.

Since I live remotely and use mobile Wi-Fi-based internet, this is not an option for me, but I have met several people who use their home service via mobile devices to watch their satellite or cable TV channels while living the mobile lifestyle part of the year. I have used both Dish Network and Direct TV during my mobile lifestyle in my travel trailer. It basically comes down to preference. Just like the cell phone companies, they all suck, but they get away with it when they are the only game in town.

One last piece of information: if you have satellite TV from Dish Network or Direct TV at home, you can add an RV package for a nominal fee. It used to be you had to have two separate accounts, but now you can just have one account with an additional fee.

Also at the time I write this, you can freeze your RV account if you only travel part of the year, thereby not having to pay for both active accounts. You can also freeze your home account for six months the last time I checked. The problem is, if you freeze your home account, you cannot use your added RV account. I'm not sure if this is always the case, but it seems to change often and it depends on who you talk to in customer service.

MOBILE INTERNET ACCESS

Having mobile internet access has been a must for me because I run my business remotely. For some, this will not be important, but it can be critical if you need to make a living via the web.

Just like mobile TV, there are numerous options for mobile internet. Today, satellite TV providers usually have their own service or they have a partnership with a satellite internet service. At this time, this will require separate equipment ranging from a few hundred dollars to several thousand. If you are truly in remote areas, satellite internet will more than likely be your only option.

Luckily today, with expanded cell phone tower coverage, most cell phone providers, depending where you are, have Wi-Fi coverage for internet access. Over the years, this is what I have primarily used for my internet access. At this time, I use a combination of my smartphone and an external Wi-Fi device through Verizon. At times, I have had spotty coverage, but for the most part, it has worked just fine. Remember, I run my business remotely and have for several years. Also, most RV parks have free Wi-Fi, or will provide Wi-Fi access for an additional fee.

As you can see, living a pretty normal lifestyle in a mobile setting is doable with today's technology. Don't get me wrong, it's not perfect, but I think the downside is well worth the upside.

WASHER AND DRYER

Yes, you read that correctly! Today's modern fifth-wheels and Class A motorhomes can come equipped with a stackable or all-in-one washer and dryer. As a matter of fact, a lot of the bigger ones come with washer and dryer hookups as a standard option. My parents own a 2007 fifth-wheel and it has washer and dryer hookups. As I write this, it is over ten years old.

I have not seen a travel trailer that has a washer and dryer hookups. This is not to say they don't exist, but I have never seen one and I have looked at a lot of travel trailers.

DISHWASHER

Having a dishwasher is a pretty common option in fifth-wheels and Class A motor homes today. In fact, I have seen Class A and fifth-wheel kitchens that would rival million-dollar homes. I kid you not, some I have seen are pretty incredible.

Now there are a ton of other creature comfort options, such as big screen TVs and reclining lounge chairs, but I think you can see now the RV of today is no joke. Even standard equipment RVs come with a lot of goodies these days; they just keep getting better and better.

11

RV Maintenance

You must remember, your RV is basically a miniature house, but because it rolls it will require the maintenance of both a home and an automobile all rolled into one. Below I will outline some of the most common maintenance items that apply when owning a RV.

BASIC TOOLS

One thing I would definitely recommend is to carry a basic set of tools with you. I personally have a decent of tools in a toolbox in my truck, and then another set of basic home maintenance tools in my travel trailer. What would a basic set of tools look like? Here's my list of the things I carry:

- Tire air pressure gauge

- Air pump with 150psi capabilities. Big trucks have big tires; a little pump is not going to do the job

- Screwdriver set

- Shovel (if you get stuck, this is a life saver)
- Various wrenches, standard and metric
- Socket set, standard and metric
- Extra-large crescent wrench
- Hammer
- Cordless drill
- Drill bits
- Hacksaw
- Pliers
- Wire strippers
- Lubricating/penetrating oil
- Duct tape
- Electrical tape
- Silicone caulk
- Various size alkaline batteries
- Car battery charger
- Jumper cables
- Crazy Glue
- Zip ties
- Bailing wire
- Hose clamps

- Rags

- First aid kit

- Fire extinguisher(s)

This isn't an all-inclusive tool list, but this should be enough to fix a lot of issues that may arise.

COMMON RV MAINTENANCE

This isn't an all-inclusive maintenance list, but below are the most common do-it-yourself (DIY) tasks. Some of these, like oil changes, you may wish to have someone else do. Depending on where you are located, there are mobile RV service mechanics who will come to you to do basic maintenance and repairs. Always check your RV owner's manual for a detailed maintenance list.

- Check tire pressure and make sure lug nuts are tight on the tow vehicle and RV every time you hit the road.

- If your RV is motorized, basic oil changes every 3,500 to 5,000 miles and check air filters.

- If you use a mobile or self-contained generator, change oil per operator manual recommendations.

- RVs have various external seams with rubberized sealer that should be checked every six months.

- Regularly check your roof for any wear, tear, or possible leaks.

- Have your brakes checked regularly on both the tow vehicle and RV.

- Travel trailer and fifth-wheel axle bearings need to be checked and regreased every 5,000 to 10,000 miles. Make sure to check your owner's manual for specifics.

- Check blinkers, brake, and towing lights before you go on the road.

- Flush black water holding tank on a regular basis.

- Winterize your RV when storing; check owner's manual for specifics on your model of RV.

12

What to Expect Living the Mobile Lifestyle

Now that you have the basic information about the mobile lifestyle and what the various RV options are, I want to tell you what to expect out of the lifestyle.

In one word: FREEDOM!

I know this lifestyle is not for everyone, but for those of you who are getting fired up about possibly starting this life adventure, I want to spend a little time explaining the freedom and benefits that come along with the lifestyle from my perspective.

PURE MOBILITY

I honestly kick myself for not starting the mobile lifestyle much earlier in my life. Think about it—you can go almost anywhere at any given time! Let that truly sink in . . . I know it's a little overwhelming at first.

I still remember the first night in my first travel trailer thinking, I have nothing tying me down. I can back up my truck, hook up the trailer, and boom!—I'm gone. In a strange sense, I was returning to my roots as a hunter-gatherer, but with all the modern creature comforts. The best part is I didn't have to worry about a bear or mountain lion trying to eat me . . . well not completely, I guess.

This is going to be a completely different lifestyle than what you have been living in the past, so take your time. There will be several lessons that you will learn along the way, some painful; just be ready for when they occur.

You will also be exposed to an entire new group of like-minded people who are on their own journeys. Not a day goes by where I don't run into someone doing the same thing, ready to discuss how they are doing it and what their future plans are. I will say this, just like the off-the-gridders, they are some of the nicest people I have met—and always willing to lend a helping hand or give some free advice.

Bye-Bye, Bad Neighbor

How many of us have had that neighbor that we try to avoid at all cost? You know the one, always coming over to borrow your tools to never return them, throwing parties at all hours of the night, parking in front of your house to keep their driveway open, allowing their pets to relieve themselves in your front yard . . . you get the point. We've all had them. I know I've had my fair share of them, and there is nothing worse than realizing you are stuck with them, unless you or they move. Pretty difficult to do when you own a home, not to mention expensive and stressful.

With the mobile lifestyle, a move is as quick as backing up your vehicle, hooking up your trailer, firing up that Class A, B, or C motor home, and getting out of Dodge. As an example, I was staying at an RV park a couple of years ago and had a complete human skidmark of a neighbor. Not only was he extremely disrespectful to everyone around him, but he was also flat-out dangerous. In today's residential neighborhoods, this would be an absolute disaster. There was no better feeling than just packing my stuff up in an hour and leaving. This was the only time this has happened. The owners of the RV resort were way too lenient, which is definitely the exception and not the rule. Most RV resorts do not put up with any crap, and the people who stay at them are usually very easy to get along with.

Here 's the kicker: in a lot of RV resorts, you will actually have more space between you and your neighbor than today's typical neighborhood.

THINGS WILL CHANGE

As with all things in life, circumstances change. When I first started out, I was just going to use my travel trailer as a go-between while waiting to finish my off-the-grid house. Once I started living the lifestyle, though, I absolutely fell in love with it. My first travel trailer had only the basics, just enough to get by. But once I realized I wanted to explore this type of life a little more, I realized I would need to get a travel trailer that would better fit where I was going in the future. I had no idea that I would live both an off-the-grid and mobile lifestyle, but that is what eventually happened.

I'll tell you this, it is not uncommon for people living this type of lifestyle to upgrade and go through various RVs. So don't feel discouraged if your first one doesn't seem to be the right fit a year later. I would just plan on it happening at some point. You may start off single, get married, have kids, acquire some pets, or the reverse may happen and you may become an empty nester. The best part is, no matter where you are in your life, as far as goals and living situation, there is an RV for you.

Heck, I'm looking at making another jump and purchasing my fourth travel trailer in this ever-continuing adventure. I'm guessing this will not be my last RV either; I'm sure down the road things will change and I'll get another one(s). Now try doing the same thing with a house . . . ain't gonna happen unless you are a talented property flipper.

FINAL THOUGHTS

As you can now see, this mobile lifestyle has a lot of intricate pieces that you must learn in the beginning, but that's life in general. Everything I have done in life that resulted in more freedom and success has come with some scrapes and bruises along the way. A few famous sayings come to mind when I think of the above:

> *If it was easy, everyone would be doing it!*
> *How do you eat an elephant? . . . One bite at a time!*

For me, the lessons, good and bad, have been well worth it, and I'm definitely glad I made the leap into this type of life. I hope this book gives you some real-life insight to what mobile living really means, and if you decide to go into this adventure, I hope I've made your transition easier. Trust me, writing books is hard work, so I don't do this just for fun. It's important to me to share the positive and sometimes negative things I have learned in life.

How I live, the books I write, and the information I share comes purely from the heart. I consider myself to be incredibly fortunate both to live the life I do and to know a lot of people who share my same passions. This type of life has brought me into contact with people I would not have met otherwise, and that is one of the biggest rewards I have received. When you're around like-minded people with similar goals, life just seems to be better.

With that said, always feel free to reach out and contact me. I'm an odd bird in the writing, self-improvement, and life simplification world because I answer all my emails personally. I know there may come a day when I can't do this, but I sure hope not. Being around people with similar interests and passions, makes what I do pure bliss . . . Heck, I don't even consider it work at times.

If there is one main point of emphasis I can leave with you it is to do what you are passionate about and follow your dreams. It sounds cheesy and rah-rah (imagine some cheerleader with pom-poms), but I can tell you firsthand, it is really that simple and straightforward.

I hope to run into you on the road someday, and maybe even have an adult beverage and share some stories. Thanks again for taking the time to read this book, and I wish you the best in all your life's adventures.

Gary Collins

Did You Enjoy This Book? You Can Make a Big Difference and Spread the Word!

Reviews are the most powerful tool I have to bring attention to *The Simple Life*. I'm an independently published author and yes, I do a lot of this work myself. This helps me make sure the information I provide is straight from the heart and comes from my experiences without some publishing company dictating what sells. You, the readers, are my muscle and marketing machine.

You are a committed group and a loyal bunch of fans!

I truly love my fans and the passion they have for my writing and products. Simply put, your reviews help bring more fans to my books and attention to what I'm trying to teach.

If you liked this book, or any of my others for that matter, I would be very grateful if you would spend a couple of minutes and leave a review. Doesn't have to be long, just something conveying your thoughts.

Please visit Amazon.com to leave a review for my book(s).

Thank you!

ABOUT GARY

Gary Collins, MS, was raised in the High Desert at the basin of the Sierra Nevada mountain range in a rural part of California. He now lives part of the year in a remote area of northeast Washington State, and the other part of the year is dedicated to exploring in his travel trailer with his trusty black lab Barney.

Gary considers himself lucky to have grown up in a very small town experiencing fishing, hunting, and anything outdoors from a very young age. He has been involved in organized sports, nutrition, and fitness for almost four decades. He is also an active follower and teacher of what he calls "life simplification." He believes that *"Today we're bombarded by too much stress, and not enough time for personal fulfillment. We're failing to take care of our health and be truly happy . . . there has to be a better way!"*

Collins' background is very unique and brings a much-needed perspective to today's conversations about health, nutrition, entrepreneurship, self-help and self-reliance. He holds an AS degree in Exercise Science, a BS in Criminal Justice, and an MS in Forensic Science.

He has a unique and interesting background that includes

military intelligence, and roles as a Special Agent for the US State Department Diplomatic Security Service, the US Department of Health and Human Services, and the US Food and Drug Administration.

In addition to being a best-selling author, Gary has taught at the university level, consulted and trained college-level athletes, and been interviewed for his expertise on various subjects by *CBS Sports*, *Coast to Coast AM*, *The RT Network*, and *FOX News* to name a few.

The Simple Life website and book series (his total lifestyle reboot), blows the lid off conventional life and wellness expectations, and is essential for every person seeking a simpler and better life.

For more information about his publications and services go to: www.thesimplelifenow.com.

REFERENCES

"Air Suspension Basics for Towing." *Truck Trend*, 29 July 2016, www.trucktrend.com/how-to/chassis-suspension/1607-air-suspension-basics-for-towing/

California Department of Motor Vehicles. *Recreational Trailer Endorsement*, www.dmv.ca.gov

www.census.gov/construction/nrs/pdf/uspricemon.pdf

"Ford Motor Company Timeline." *Ford Corporate*, corporate. www.ford.com/history.html

www.gorving.com

Harris, William. "How Motorcycles Work." *HowStuffWorks*, HowStuffWorks, 18 Nov. 2005, www.auto.howstuffworks.com/motorcycle6.htm

Morrison, Jim. "Commemorating 100 Years of the RV." *Smithsonian.com*, Smithsonian Institution, 24 Aug. 2010, www.smithsonianmag.com/history/commemorating-100-years-of-the-rv-56915006/

Vehicles, California Department of Motor. *Recreational Trailer Endorsement*, www.dmv.ca.gov

www.ycharts.com/indicators/sales_price_of_existing_homes